soul-ITUDE

FINDING PEACE
for the
STRESSED-OUT SOUL

TODD & JEDD HAFER

Published in Boise, Idaho, by Elevate Faith,
an imprint of Elevate Publishing.

ISBN: 9781945449222
E-Book ISBN: 9781945449222
LOC Control Number: 2016955891

I am leaving you with a gift—
peace of mind and heart. And
the peace I give is a gift the
world cannot give. So don't
be troubled or afraid.

John 14:27

NEW LIVING TRANSLATION

A special thanks to Matt Dragon
for inspiring and road-testing
many of the ideas in this book.

PUBLISHER'S NOTE

Many years ago, as I was finishing graduate school and preparing to get married, I decided to fast from solid food for 40 days. The majority of that time I spent at a retreat center in rural Illinois. I was the only person in residence the entire time I was there.

Ever since then, life has felt like a rush of activity that continues to intensify. In one sense, I am a serious fan of technology. It enables me to have a lot of flexibility with my life as well as to grow our business in a non-geographically limited way. But I've noticed that in many ways, I feel like I have paradoxically become enslaved in my search for more freedom. Enslaved to society's expectations of immediate response, my own developed desire to be constantly updated on the latest development, and keeping up with life that moves at the speed of light. Or faster.

As I reflect on my life, there is very little I would change. I love my work. I love my wife, Laurie. I love our kids, Noah and Anastasia. We are busy. Very busy. But we have long since removed the unnecessary from our lives and are almost purely focused on the activities that we feel are a high priority.

A few years ago, that was not the case, and I had to cut back on everything extracurricular. Much of it was good and noble: serving on nonprofit boards, engaging in charity, and speaking regularly at our local church. But the pace of life and the growing amount of to-do's meant something had to go. We had to make decisions.

Many days, I close my eyes and long to be back at that retreat center in Illinois with nothing to do but pray, meditate, and read. Life was so pure and simple.

But that's not realistic anymore, and that's more than okay. I could never live 40 days without Laurie, Noah, and Anastasia. Going without food would be so much easier. Nevertheless, I have learned that I need to be refreshed, rested, and restored for both my family and our company. To achieve that, I have had to learn how to relive those 40 days at the retreat center along the path of life. Without that, my soul would be depleted.

A while back, I sat in a restaurant with Jedd Hafer, and we talked about how our souls needed to be energized daily, weekly, and annually, just like our bodies. It was out of that conversation that the idea of this book was born. I am thankful to Todd and Jedd for running with the idea and listing so many of the reasons why our stressed-out souls need to find peace, along with an exceptionally helpful list of practical ways to achieve that.

May this book help you, in your search to keep the pace of contemporary life, to find peace in a soulful way.

Mark Russell

CEO, ELEVATE PUBLISHING

SOLITUDE AND BEAUTY CAN HEAL THE SOUL!

In a world where people are constantly bombarded with more stimulation and are often "left to their own devices," here is an incredible secret of some of the happiest people you know: **SOLITUDE**. They get away. Away from the noise, from the chaos, and from the hustle.

Jesus did it (a lot). Some of the wisest and most productive people in the world insist on it.

We hope this book will help you get away and find a sense of stillness in the beauty of creation. Our goal is to help you be more intentional about shutting out the noise and the constant, frenetic motion of our society. Then you will be able to implement the practical ideas to lower stress.

If you are overstressed and overstimulated by the frantic pace of this modern world, this book is meant to encourage, soothe, inspire, and instruct.

You don't need all the flash and noise society offers in order to be content. You CAN find peace outside in creation, breathing fresh air. You just need a quiet place where you can listen. With this project, we hope to steer you toward solitude and rest for your soul. May peace be with you.

Todd & Jedd Hafer

When you arise in the morning,
think of what a precious privilege
it is to be alive—to breathe,
to think, to enjoy, to love.

MARCUS AURELIUS

Finally, brothers and sisters,
whatever is true, whatever is
noble, whatever is right, whatever
is pure, whatever is lovely,
whatever is admirable—if anything
is excellent or praiseworthy—
think about such things.

PHILIPPIANS 4:8 (NIV)

Slow me down, Lord. Ease the pounding of my heart by the quieting of my mind.

COWBOY PRAYER

SLOW IT ALL DOWN...

Did you know that you make *612 conscious decisions per day?* That is a lot of work. Your senses take in as much as four quadrillion bytes of information per second.

You are completely flooded with information. Your brain must constantly ignore and set aside massive amounts of data. Still, you are confronted nonstop with "interruptions"—things that seemingly must be dealt with RIGHT NOW.

You are bombarded with the urgent, but how much of it truly qualifies?

How can you give your mind some needed rest? First, you must *decide* that rest is important. You must give your mind permission.

We are made in God's image, right? Well, He rested through one-seventh of the process of creating the world. Perhaps, then, we can start by giving ourselves permission to slow down and rest. Maybe you can start to shake the myth that you must be in constant motion to be "productive" (and therefore, important).

True, the quest to "bear fruit" is important. But one of the essential "fruits" our lives are meant to produce is PEACE. As you look around, do you see many peaceful people? Or, as you blitz through your day, do you see frantic, overstressed, frustrated people everywhere?

You can set yourself apart. As everyone else is bouncing around, you can be grounded and still—if you *allow* yourself to soak in the wisdom of slowing down.

Tell yourself that resting IS an important part of your life. Give yourself permission to slow down, take your time, and look at something beautiful. You are NOT wasting that time. Assure yourself that you are, in fact, spending it wisely.

The Bible talks about REST and PEACE more than most people realize. It is almost as if the Guy who created your mind and body knew a few things. Constant stress and constant fast-paced activity destroy. Your body needs a time of recovery and rest. Taking good care of your machine is good stewardship. Taking good care of your body and mind does not equal laziness! It equals wisdom.

Is your life a race when it should really be a journey? And, is your journey carrying you in the right direction? That depends. Is your journey bringing you closer to what, and who, makes you feel most alive?

The Lord is my shepherd,
I lack nothing.

He makes me lie down
in green pastures,

He leads me beside quiet waters,
He refreshes my soul.

He guides me along the right paths
for His name's sake.

PSALM 23:1-3 (NIV)

Goodness is the only investment
that never fails.

HENRY DAVID THOREAU

RARE AIR

Consider this:

Oxygen is life. Without breath, we are not alive. Any EMT will tell you that breathing is absolutely the first priority for preserving life. And Genesis 2:1 makes it clear that we became alive when God breathed life into us.

This might seem like a silly question: Do you breathe enough?

Most people don't—they breathe too quickly and too shallowly. They breathe too much indoor air—which can be composed of an alarming amount of dead skin particles (yes, we are trying to compel you to go outside). Most people do not get enough of the miraculous exchange of pure, life-giving oxygen coming in to nourish their cells—while carbon dioxide, toxins, and waste leave their machine.

Can simply being aware of your breathing, and breathing more slowly and more deeply, actually change your stress level, your health, and ultimately your life? Absolutely, yes!

Stop right now and take this book for a walk outside. Take an oxygen supplement. Breathe in life. Take seven or eight big breaths. Nice and slow   taaaaaake your tiiiiiiimc. Now, feel it. Just feel the oxygen getting to your trillions of cells. You are alive. You are alive because God gave you your very breath. He did that because He loves you.

Hold in that air with gratitude. When it begins to feel uncomfortable, blow it all out—as much as you can. And be thankful that there is another wonderful breath waiting for you. And another one. For the rest of your life. As long as you are doing this, you are ALIVE.

Now, do you feel different? Are you glad you took the time to go outside and truly breathe?

Or, did you skip it and tell yourself, "I'll do that later"? If so, do it now. Unless you are reading this on an airplane. In that case, you are excused until you are safely outside of the terminal.

BREATHING— SCIENCE STUFF

Here's what you recently accomplished with all that breathing and why it is awesome:

According to scientists (the smart ones—not the ones who are wrong all the time), you have just created a calming effect on your entire nervous system. You have released tension in your muscles and lowered your blood pressure. You have also triggered positive results in your brain, digestive system, lymphatic system, and immune system. Breathing in a slow, controlled, *intentional* manner changes the response of your body's autonomic nervous system which (without your knowledge) controls other systems like digestion and circulation. Breathing is linked to these systems. And it is impossible to relax these without breathing more slowly (and taking in more oxygen). It is also *impossible* to breathe in this manner and miss the desired benefits on these systems.

When you focus on and control your breathing, you are unleashing AUTOMATIC positive effects throughout your physical body.

And we haven't even touched on what you are doing for your mind. Because your mind and body are LINKED. As your body relaxes, your mind calms.

We know this is true because we have discovered neurochemicals and the parasympathetic branch of the nervous system. Neurochemicals send signals to tell your body how to feel. Basically, when you breathe this way, your brain gets a message that all is well and your body responds involuntarily.

In a recent study of people with major depression, after 12 weeks of regular coherent breathing (in this case, in a yoga class), the participants showed a significant increase in gamma-aminobutyric acid (GABA), a brain chemical associated with calming and antianxiety effects. More than that, participants reported that their anxiety and depressive symptoms decreased![1]

What does all this science stuff mean? Slow, deep, intentional breathing is one of the best things you can do for your body and your mind. And it WILL reduce the negative effects of stress on your body.

Treat Your Body Like It Belongs
to Someone You Love.

LIFE MOVING TOO FAST?
TIME TO FAST.

Have you ever tried fasting? How about fasting from something besides food—such as your smartphone? If that sounds crazy, consider that you have put yourself in a position where you cannot go without something that didn't exist 20 years ago.

You didn't have an Internet-enabled device in your hands 20 years ago. Or a way to stay in touch with virtually every person you know, every second. How did you live?

In a world where we are often "left to our own devices," we are clearly LESS peaceful and MORE stressed than ever. If that device in our hands contained all the answers to peace and happiness, why are depression and anxiety meds being prescribed at skyrocketing rates? The fact is that the stimulus of being "connected" (some would argue that, as human beings, we are truly *less* connected than ever) can be a harmful addiction. It can sap our energy and our actual productivity.

More and more, we are seeing this compulsive device behavior as a destructive addiction. You know how devastating it can be to your time and productivity.

This trend can also wreak havoc in our relationships. We stay in our own little world as our connection to real, live people suffers—very different from the solitude we are hoping to achieve. Solitude is NOT putting ourselves in an electronic trance where we are LESS aware of ourselves and our surroundings.

In fact, to become more aware of ourselves and our beautiful world, some version of electronic device fasting is ESSENTIAL.

Here are a few fasting options that have worked for other people. (They can work for you too, and they won't kill you.)

- Go for a walk and leave your phone at home. On purpose. While you're outside, you can notice that the Earth is still spinning and life as we know it has not ended. You might NOTICE A LOT MORE when not staring down at a screen.

- Put your phone away (out of sight) when in the presence of your loved ones. You will enjoy better face-to-face interaction (you know, the way we were made to interact). It works best when you ask loved ones to do the same. If this seems overwhelming, pick a time to do it. Some families reserve this policy for dinner or all meal times. Our friends at the Love and Logic Institute[2] started a wonderful trend called Phone Down Friday (#PhoneDown-Friday #PDF) in which a day of the week (it doesn't have to be Friday) is reserved for paying more attention to loved ones' faces and less attention to screens and devices. They even give parents a great line to use with their kids: "Time with you is important, so I'm putting my phone away while we're talking. Thank you for doing the same."

- Go on a long hike or visit a place in nature (you'll be encouraged to do things like this throughout the book) and [gulp] DON'T BRING YOUR PHONE. Now, obviously, we want you to use some common sense and be sure to stay safe. This may include going with someone, letting people know where you'll be, going to a familiar area, or even bringing the device and just vowing to leave it zipped in a pocket. Or go to a place with spotty, frustrating service so you won't be tempted.

- While you are at work or at home, set a timer and see how long you can go without looking at your device. When you look, stop the timer. Now, try to beat your own record.

- Pick a time of day that you DO return emails and texts. This can be a long-term solution, as it will start to train people when to expect answers. This practice will actually increase your productivity as constant interruptions decrease and your focus increases.

- Experiment with apps and settings that notify people you are unavailable (driving or otherwise—these can save lives). In addition, you can let people know via social media, your contacts, or even actual conversing that you will be fasting from electronics. For extra credit, challenge them to do the same. This can be used in concert with the previous hint and once again "train" your contacts that you have set times for returning messages.

- When in a time of prayer, meditation, or sleep, DO NOT have a phone or similar device in the room.

- Go completely "dark" and live 100 percent off the grid. (If you know how to accomplish this, please contact us—wait, never mind). [Wink]

Take your eyes off what the world
is doing and turn your thoughts
inward—and upward.
It **WILL** be worth it.

Almost everything will work again
if you unplug it for a few minutes…
including you.

ANNE LAMOTT

If you truly love nature, you will
find beauty everywhere.

VINCENT VAN GOGH

THE POWER OF SPACE

This may not sound like good news to some, but occupying space alone in your room is NOT the same as exploring *outside.* There is something very special about getting away from the walls, the structures, the noise, and, yes, the people all around you.

Experiencing the vastness of the night sky, the top of a mountain, or a nature trail inspires us to consider God.

Neuroscientists have discovered that the farther you shift your focus away from yourself (say, to the stars) and toward an *expansive view*, the more awe you will feel. This act triggers a "religious experience" response in your brain's parietal lobes. Psychologists have noted that when you change your physical location, it has an undeniable impact on the way you feel. Combine these two facts and you begin to understand the powerful effect of getting out, away, and to a place where you can take in an awesome view.

Think about that: Once again, going from an enclosed, indoor "prison" to the open air and viewing the sky lowers your stress. It changes your outlook, literally and figuratively. Not to mention the benefits of breathing in fresh air to your physical body!

What if it's cold outside? Being from Colorado, we know the answer to that: Wear more **layers**.

Yes, we can conjure all kinds of excuses to avoid venturing to the beautiful, amazing outdoors (weather, allergies, lack of time). But if we make it a priority, we can muster the means (a jacket or an allergy pill) and the will to get out there.

Solitude helps you discover
what you believe in.

Contemplation allows you
to believe (and live) what
you have discovered.

TODD HAFER

SOLITUDE VS. ISOLATION

(Spoiler: Solitude kicks Isolation's rear)

Solitude is not *isolation.* Unfortunately, in our modern world, we get plenty of isolation. Commuting in our cars or even on a crowded train or plane. We tend to be isolated via the exclusive personal stimulus of our electronic devices. Being glued to the screen of a phone or tablet, loading up on stimuli and artificially messing with our hormones (you get a dopamine rush every time you win a game or even get a text—and it becomes addictive), is NOT solitude! It's not even a good escape. We weren't made that way. We were created as *relational* creatures. We are designed to relate to one another face-to-face.

When we see a baby, we make eye contact, we smile, and we might coo (some of us have been known to lose IQ points in the presence of babies). This is foundational communication—the way we were made to relate to one another! How much of that do we get in our adult interactions? Not enough.

THE WAY WE ARE MADE

Let's be very frank. We were made to move, and we don't move enough. We were made to walk outside. We don't do that enough. We were made to relate face-to-face, and we don't do that enough. And we were made to move and physically work. We don't do that enough. We live a life that too often ignores the way we were made.

We were also made to stand in awe of creation, to feel our smallness in contrast with the awesomeness of God and His creative power. We certainly don't do that enough! The practice of solitude and limiting artificial distractions will make you more aware of your connection with God.

This is a guarantee: If your lifestyle reflects the way you were created, you WILL feel more in touch with your CREATOR.

Wait, I thought you just said…

Okay, there seems to be a contradiction here, doesn't there? We were talking about *solitude*. Then we stated that we are created to be in relationship with others. Well, which is it? [Foot tapping in a demanding rhythm…]

Both. We need solitude so that we can be *better* for those relationships. Getting in touch with creation, our Creator, and our*selves* will help us appreciate and navigate our other relationships.

DANGEROUS SOLITUDE

We should note that solitude can be dangerous. It can feel so good, so relaxing, and so freeing that we may be tempted to overdo it. We may be tempted to substitute solitude for those fulfilling relational moments. But we must remember that BOTH things are important. Just as there is a time for rest and a time for activity, there is a time for community and a time for aloneness.

HUMANS DO NOT LIVE BY SOLITUDE ALONE.

If you find yourself struggling to come back to the community end of the continuum, take somebody you love and **share the majesty you've found out there.** *Share* **the beauty and stillness of a quiet, isolated place.**

Few things are better than helping a loved one find the peace and relaxation you found you have discovered. This *can* be done together, and we promise you will not be a walking (or hiking) oxymoron.

First, keep peace within
yourself; then you can also
bring peace to others.

THOMAS À KEMPIS

Every day we are called to do
small things with great love.

MOTHER TERESA

COMPARISON STINKS—COMPARED TO NOT COMPARING...

Solitude's benefits are almost limitless. But here's a big one: Solitude frees us from the trap of comparison and competition. Comparison can create a ton of stress in our lives. See what Jedd says here (in his *epic* book on stress—which has sold well under a million copies) about the "keeping up with the Joneses" belief:

> *"Most of us have pounded into us from the time we are tiny what I call the **'Keeping Up with the Joneses' belief** (myth). Sadly, too many people buy into this idea (pun intended), and it causes more stress than just about anything.*

Deconstructing This Dangerous Belief:
Reflect on your life. Remember when____had that type of notebook, acid-wash jeans, tennis shoes, car—whatever? And if you didn't, you'd be an outcast and die? What do you think about those items now? Many advertisers still see it as their job to make you believe that the Joneses are happy and you are not—all because they have___ and you don't. Garbage!

> *Unfortunately, we are susceptible. We all believe having that stuff will make us happier—at least a little bit. And we could all lower our bad stress by intentionally refusing to buy into that nonsense.*

And it is nonsense. In addition to the fact that subscribing to this belief will add to your stress more than anything else—it's also flat wrong.

Stuff isn't happiness! *Stuff is fleeting. Stuff is, most often, obsolete by the time the limited warranty expires. Stuff you were dying to have a few years ago is now in a bag for Goodwill. The 'Keeping Up with the Joneses' belief is a recipe for discontent, overspending, and a lack of enjoyment. Be thankful for what you have and ignore the voice (it's on your TV, tablet, or radio right now) that happiness comes in the form of some new product.*

*Stop believing it! Make the choice. I wish it were a simple matter of pulling out the 'Keeping Up with the Joneses' chip and popping in the 'Stuff Doesn't Matter' or the 'Gratefulness' chip. But you do have some control over which beliefs you choose to adopt and reinforce when it comes to material things. You also have access to thousands of celebrity stories in which they had all the Joneses could ever want and more—yet they turned to drugs and even suicide to **escape the stress.** Better still, you have access to real people, and stories of real people, who live **joyful lives despite unbelievably tragic circumstances.***" [3]
[Excerpted from *Shrink Your Stress in 5 Steps* by Jedd Hafer, *Amazon.com,* 2014]

This brings us to a great benefit of solitude:

When you are experiencing it, there is NOBODY around to compare yourself to.

We can't say enough about the damaging effects of constantly looking around and comparing yourself to others.

Think about it—the only two real possibilities are:

1. You feel like you are better than others. This is bad.

2. You feel worse than others. This is bad.

We are not saying there is no place in this world for competition, for sharpening one another, or pushing one another to strive. What we're talking about here is the maddening, stress-inducing roller coaster of "How does my life compare to _____'s?"

It happens on social media all the time. Remember social media? Like anything else, it can be used for evil or for good. You probably have friends and family who spend most of their time on social media complaining about everything. They may have forgotten the many blessings that are evident in their lives—if only they would appreciate them.

Then, there are those *other* friends who seem to be continuously advertising "Look How Awesome Our Life Is Every Day, All The Time!"

A little disgusting sometimes? But how many of us get sucked into this trap: "Why am I not that _____ (happy, wealthy, skinny, attractive, good at photographing my delicious food)?"

It's a recipe for discontent.

These Facebook friends may not mean to steal your contentment, but that's what happens. (Note: We know that it's the *advertisers'* job to steal our contentment.)

This brings us to another benefit of solitude. It allows us to escape from advertisers—and their number-one tool: Boom!—COMPARISON.

Often, it's the before-and-after in which YOU are the "before."

"And if you buy this, you'll be happy and successful like THIS actor who is portraying a real person."

To seek solitude is to seek a break from all of that input indigestion we get when we are bombarded with images of how we "should be."

We submit that you are *much* more likely to get glimpses of a wonderful reality when you go for a walk (with no device) than you would parked on social media. You'll be taking a break from manipulative, potentially damaging messages—and opening yourself up to hearing and understanding yourself and God better.

But I have quieted my heart...

KING DAVID

Love is the greatest beautifier
in the universe.

MAY CHRISTIE

CHOOSING LIFE

Life can be all about choices. In order to be more intentional about finding peace and happiness, consider some of these simple daily choices:

Outdoors vs. Indoors

Looking at something lovely vs. Staring at a screen

Parking far away vs. Fighting for a close spot

Thankfulness vs. Covetousness and want

Listening vs. Ranting

Reading vs. Watching TV

Meditation vs. Playing video games

Appreciating vs. Worrying

Slowness and stillness vs. Hurry

Simple vs. Complicated

Fresh food vs. Junk food

Water vs. Soda or alcohol

Prayer vs. Junk social media

Scripture vs. Entertainment

Is it possible that peace exists
inside of us, but our minds are
often too loud to hear it?

MATT DRAGON

TAKE A HIKE

Doctors are now saying that hiking can actually alter your brain (in a good way).

We've known for a while that moderately vigorous exercise has endless physical benefits (such as burning 400–700 calories per hour, increasing circulation, burning fat, and boosting essential vitamin D). But doctors are beginning to "prescribe" hiking outdoors specifically for patients with mental health issues. Why? It reduces *rumination*—the continuous focus on troubling or worrisome thoughts. Focusing on these bad thoughts can feed anxiety and depression. Research has found that hiking in creation reduces the focus on negative thoughts, and even the simple change in location is a powerful tool to **change mood**. There's even a recently coined term for this—*ecotherapy*.

Hiking in nature decreases these negative or depressing thoughts while boosting cognitive function and creative problem-solving. It can relieve stress and release endorphins (feel-good chemicals).

In a 2013 study in the UK, researchers found that people who went to "green spaces" (outdoors where there are magical things like grass and trees—and a lack of buildings and recycled air) experienced more relaxed feelings and more positive emotions overall.

It is a guarantee that after just 10 minutes of walking outside, you WILL feel different (let's call it "better") than you did before you left. And 10 minutes each day can be life-changing for people with physical and mental health challenges.

You don't have to trek for a long time. You don't have to hike very far. You don't need a lot of special gear. Just get out there and do your body and brain some good.

There is pleasure in
the pathless woods.

LORD BYRON

PACE—THE POWER OF ACCEPTING A SLOWER CADENCE

One of today's biggest myths is that if you don't get results *right away*, something's not working. We are so addicted to immediate gratification, immediate answers, and immediate results. We want to put everything in the microwave.

When kids don't know something, what do they do? If you said "Google it," you haven't been around *our* kids. They ask their parents first because that's faster. Then, in the *highly* unlikely event we don't know, they roll their eyes like slot machines and sigh—*now* they have to Google it. Now they have to go through the arduous ordeal of asking their device that will span the virtual universe in seconds and get them any answer. Don't they have it rough?

But on many levels, we know this lifestyle is not healthy for them. We know searching for answers can help us appreciate those answers more. We know that working and struggling for things is an antidote for entitlement. We know that patience and self-control are good.

You might have read about the studies in which marshmallows were placed in front of children and the children were told, "You can have ONE marshmallow right now, or you can wait and you get to have this whole bag."

Then, the researchers followed these kids through life.

The kids who could patiently delay "marshmallow gratification" did better in school, careers, and relationships, as well as in other areas of life by just about every measure (including SAT scores and body mass index).[4]

You get the idea. People who can slow down, delay, be patient, and wait for the marshmallow tend to do better in life and enjoy it more.

If we ran the world (don't hold your breath), every kid would be required to grow something. Each child would have to get a little cup of good dirt and push a little seed down into it. They would be required to water it the first day and to watch.

Nothing. They would go back the next day. Still nothing. Water it some more. A few days later—a tiny little green sprout. They would watch it grow as the days moved by. They would understand the miraculous, remarkably slow process and its value. And they would understand that some things CANNOT BE RUSHED.

Too many things are rushed already in our world, and that is not good.

You know that when you rush, you make more mistakes. You enjoy less. You feel more adrenocorticotropic hormone and cortisol (i.e., *stress*) pumping through your body. You know that when you are calm, you think and reason better.

Sometimes, keeping that fast pace can make us feel important. It can make us feel alive. But, it's an illusion. There is an emphasis in our modern society on being the fastest. Speed doesn't necessarily mean we are getting things done—or done well.

Speed is not everything. It takes a glacier a year to move as far as you can walk in five minutes. But, eventually, glaciers carve canyons and mold mountains. Slow movement can change the world. Perseverance can change the world. So can you.

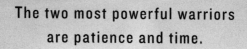

The two most powerful warriors
are patience and time.

LEO TOLSTOY

WILL WORK FOR PEACE:

Daily Habits to Benefit Your Soul

Life is composed of days. Days that tend to fly by. And days are made up of moments. Let's talk about some key moments in each of your days.

Those moments when you wake up and stretch, take some deep breaths, drink some water (preferably with some fresh lemon), do some pushups or yoga poses, pray, read your devotions, think about things for which you are thankful, drink coffee or tea, and feel alive. Smile at somebody you love—even your own face in the mirror. Go outside, lean back, and smile up at the sky. Not enough of these moments? You can change that right away with relative ease.

Your best life will always be made up of the things you do every day. And your best path to spiritual and physical health will be driven by the habits you *install* in your days. One of the greatest secrets to beating stress I (Jedd) ever learned was to **link *movement* to daily habits and feelings**—the way I consistently move will become habitual and will drive the way I feel.

My insane brother Todd runs long distances—almost every day. Long ago, I stopped trying to get him professional help for this condition. I did finally ask him,

"WHY?!?" and he told me that it hurts so bad that it feels really good when he stops.

In truth, his main reason for running matches up with something powerful I discovered (and wrote about) a couple years ago. *Movement changes the way we feel.* If we want to feel different (better!) all we need to do is start moving in certain ways.

AGAIN, FROM THAT HANDY LITTLE BOOK ON STRESS:

Movement:

Your body knows some things that you don't. When you smash your finger, what do you do without thinking? Shake it vigorously? Put it in your mouth? Why? White noise.

Your brain has this cool built-in distraction system—white noise—so you don't hear the annoying noise. Think of it as your brain turning on a fan in your hotel room so you don't hear the episode of Real Housewives of New Jersey *in the next room.*

*See, your body wants to help spare you from that intense pain, so it creates **additional sensations** to drown out the noise of the pain. That's why you involuntarily shake your smashed finger. For the same reason that I sleep better when there is a fan or something running, it is a good idea to create movement and sensation when you are feeling physical symptoms of stress.*

Are you stressed right now? Try this:

Take your dominant hand and rub the back of your neck/ base of your skull for a few seconds until you feel the area warm up and relax. What happened? You created additional stimulus and you released some feel-good chemicals into your bloodstream.

*What's the key here? **If you move differently, you will feel differently.** If you want to feel better, start moving or* *change the way you are moving. In a bit, I'm going to give you more specific things you can do to change the way you feel right away. The principle of moving to feel different will come into play a lot. Just remember, move to feel better. Say it with me— "Move to feel better!"*

Honestly, very few people I've surveyed consciously do this. Almost none intentionally engage in movement to feel better— especially when they are stressed. A few get up from their desk and walk around when their tension builds. A former coworker used to rub the back of his neck and the base of his skull when he was overly stressed—but he never realized he was doing it.

Only from some of the awesome professionals I have worked with in dealing with troubled kids did I learn how powerful it could be to routinely practice self-regulation. There was a kid who practiced before court so he wouldn't freak out so bad. It wasn't just a fire drill. He was also practicing regulating himself so that when the time came, he would be successful at it.

The movement he practiced was:

1. Stand on one foot

2. Breathe deeply

We stumbled upon the balancing thing on accident. I told my genius friend Bob about how standing on one foot had really helped one of the kids calm down.

He said, "That's great use of the vestibular system of the inner ear. It is connected to the part of the brain associated with calming and regulation."

I said, "Huh?"

It turned out there was science behind the technique we had used to help kids calm down. We didn't know this at the time—but it worked anyway.

Another "trick" I stumbled upon was washing my hands. After many years in a super-stressful job running programs for troubled kids, somebody asked me why I didn't seem stressed and overwhelmed—and how I was able to prevent bringing all the pain of the job home with me. My answer was, "I wash my hands."

There was a practical reason. After high-fiving kids with questionable hygiene practices all day long, it was wise to clean my hands before picking up my children. But I also found this became a switch for me—as I washed my hands, I left the problems of work behind and transformed into "home/dad/husband/non-work guy." I still do it to this day—wash the work off my hands and symbolically let the stress of work run down the drain. Try it.

The key to effectiveness with a lot of these movements? Practice. The more you do it, the better it goes.

Want to be relaxed? Practice relaxing. What is relaxed? "Relaxed" is physical, right? Manifestations of stress are physical. High blood pressure. Weight gain. Fatigue. We don't have a body and a mind, separately. They are connected. Emotions affect our physiology. Our physical movement affects how we feel. This is why you can breathe deeply and increase the oxygen levels in your blood, lower your heart rate and blood pressure— **all without the stressor going away.**

*Why are drugs so powerful? Because the way we **feel physically** is largely chemical. There are brain chemicals that make us feel good while, at optimum balance, keeping us healthy and alive. People try all sorts of remedies for brain chemicals they think they lack. Many of these remedies are short-lived, unhealthy, ineffective, or all of the above: Sugar, caffeine, tobacco, excess alcohol, recreational drugs, thrill-seeking, unhealthy relationships, sex, pornography, electronics, etc. The list could go on.*

We know plenty of ways (from unhealthy to more healthy) to release these chemicals.

Some chemical "answers" in your body will make scientific sense. Some people find solutions through trial and error. Every physical body is different, after all.

*Ultimately, I implore you to practice **moves to make yourself feel better** before reaching for pills, medicines, drugs, drinks, and reality shows.*

*Here are some antistress **moves** that have worked for other people and happen to work for me (work is defined as making me feel good/better right away):*

***Balancing**—Be it on one foot, an exercise ball, or a balance board. I know a great teacher who used the "white noise" of ADD kids sitting on balance balls instead of chairs, with miraculous results. We also installed "the world's lowest tightrope" (piece of tape across the floor) for kids to walk when they needed to get themselves together. This was fabulous because it also employed imagination.*

Rubbing your own head and neck—This is not just about relaxing muscles or relieving physical tension (even though those things are great). People who work with troubled kids are constantly looking for appropriate self-soothing activities, and this one may go all the way back to infancy. When you cried as an infant, what happened? Right. A nice mommy or daddy person (probably Mommy—it was Daddy's turn but he didn't wake up) came and comforted you and held you. And where was her hand? Right behind your neck, supporting the base of your skull. Warm and probably stroking the back of your head. I can't prove this is why it works for me (and so many others), but I don't care. It makes me feel comforted and more relaxed. It works even better when I warm my hand first.

Rubbing lips together, chewing gum or sucking on a mint, candy, or lozenge—You can probably guess the infantile origins of this one. What's more comforting than breastfeeding? I remember it like it was yesterday. I was a big fan! Ever since Freud and his kooky friends, we have understood that oral stimulus changes the way we feel. Ask a smoker or a compulsive eater.

Rubbing your hands together briskly—A quick one you can do anywhere. I don't know why this one works so well for me. The friction creates heat and I like to be warm. It also makes a cool noise—kind of like a record scratching on a hip-hop album—go on, rub out a little Run DMC with your hands.

Good, huh? I'm partial to playing "Rockit" by Herbie Hancock. But then, I'm a master at that one. Maybe that's why it works for me—I'm good at it.

Some people also try rubbing their hands briskly over the tops of their thighs—*Be aware of your surroundings with this one. Enough said.*

Walking—*We've talked about this one. It's available to most of us most of the time, and we don't take advantage of it nearly enough. You were made to move, and this is one of the healthiest, easiest moves there is. With each step, think about some things you are thankful for—the fact that you CAN walk, the place you live, the people who love you, the sky, this amazing planet, frozen yogurt—an almost infinite list of reasons to feel grateful—even if stressful things are weighing on your mind. That sky is still awesome. You can feel better without all your problems being fixed.*

Exercise—*Mild-to-vigorous exercise has been proven to increase serotonin levels over time. Serotonin is the "feel-good" chemical. Need I say more? A few pushups or jumping jacks can make a huge difference.*

Go outside—*Coupled with mild-to-vigorous exercise, sunlight can make you feel good. Sounds like it's time for walkin' and then maybe some faster walkin', especially outside. There is also research to show that changing our location will automatically cause a change in our mood. So, especially if you feel lousy, go outside.*

Take a bath or shower—*Blood flow, relaxation, being clean, smelling better. What's not to love? If this isn't feasible, just wash your hands (see above) and maybe your face.*

Stretch, practice yoga/martial arts moves—*I really advocate doing these on your own so you can control when you do them, the duration, and the intensity. So, in this context, I'm just talking about the moves, not a class. Besides, the cost of classes might stress you out. No, seriously, there is a time and a place for a class, a trainer, a coach, somebody to push you. But I've seen classes cause problems and be stressful (running late, paying so much you feel like you're wasting money if you don't go, etc.). So, learn a few moves you can do just about anywhere, anytime.*

Laugh—*A wise woman once told me:*

> *"If you don't have anything kind and uplifting to say, you should just keep your trap shut!" There is plenty to laugh at in this life if we look for it. Give yourself permission to laugh, and don't stifle it.*

Hug somebody (with permission, please)—*Once again, this is not just me—this is research! Okay, a lot of it was my own research, but human contact is important, and we don't get enough of it. Through your iPhone doesn't count. I really did notice how much better I felt around times of physical contact with my wife (don't worry—this is not that kind of book), so I looked into it. Once again, feel-good chemicals are released* *when we hug—especially if it's for more than a second. So, look at that person you love. Hug 'em. And, we're holding... holding...*[5]

You get it. Move to feel better. And what if we don't *feel* like moving? That is why God invented the coffee bean.

Adding these "moves" will change your life. When it does, we would absolutely love for you to share your results. You might help change someone else's life, and you already know how good that feels.

We hope this book has made you smile. We hope you find some peace and solitude in this turbulent world. And we hope you will do something you love every day!

If you are looking for quick ideas:

- Put your phone away and look at your kids' or grandkids' faces.

- Walk around a park and smile at every kid or dog you see.

- Get in a kayak or canoe and paddle around the water for a bit.

- Go to a campsite and cook something over a fire. (If you can't get to one, use your barbecue grill.)

- Take a hot bath with Epsom salts and coconut oil.

- Sit outside (or at least near a window or ray of sunlight) and read a great book—if you need help finding one, try *www.elevatepub.com*.

I am not afraid of tomorrow,
for I have seen yesterday,
and I love today.

WILLIAM ALLEN WHITE

He leads me beside still waters...
He restores my soul.

PSALM 23 (ESV)

Come to me, all you who are weary and burdened, and I will give you rest. Take my yoke upon you and learn from me, for I am gentle and humble in heart, and you will find rest for your souls.

MATTHEW 11:28-29 (NIV)

Go placidly amid the noise and the haste, and remember what peace there may be in silence.

MAX EHRMANN

ABOUT THE AUTHORS

Jedd Hafer is a national speaker for the Love and Logic Institute, Inc.

Working with kids in trouble for the past 21 years, he has contributed to *Men's Health* and Lifetime Television's *Teen Trouble* with Josh Shipp. Jedd is a father of four kids (who are sometimes trouble) and has written many books with his brother Todd.

Todd Hafer is the coauthor of *Battlefield of the Mind for Teens*, an Amazon #1 Best Seller, and *City on Our Knees*, a best-selling collaboration with TobyMac. He has also written four books for the "To Save A Life" brand (which includes the $4 million movie, *To Save a Life*). Together, Todd and Jedd Hafer have written more than 50 books, sold over 2 million copies, and will speak in 25 states this year alone to audiences of more than 30,000.

PHOTOGRAPHY CREDITS:

The photography in this book, from the cover to the last page, has been provided by amateur photographers, outdoor lovers, and solitude seekers. Common people who understand the benefit and necessity of nature.

Aaron Snethen: 18, 31, 43, 49, 62, 68, 70/71, 83, 92, 123, 130

Bobby Kuber: 28, 35, 44/45, 86, 114, 124

Bryce Hafer: 15

Caedmen Bergeron: 12, 37

Courtney Link: 73, 128

Isaac Flanzbaum: 32, 52, 58, 56/57, 80/81, 88, 100/101

Jana Good: 8, 38, 50 ,65, 99, 111

Justin Rouleau: Cover, 96/97

Kasey Snethen: 95, 106/107

Kelly Borden: 17, 16/17, 66, 84/85, 91, 108, 131, 132

Kim Sutherlin: 74, 79

Rachel Rant: 20, 24

Rebecca List: 4

Rick Stratton: 127

Stephanie Kemp: 23, 27, 46, 55

ENDNOTES

[1] Findings published by *International Congress on Integrative Medicine and Health* (2016). Las Vegas, Nevada.

[2] *loveandlogic.com* or *facebook.com/loveandlogicinstitute/*

[3] Excerpted from *Shrink Your Stress in 5 Steps* by Jedd Hafer (2014). *Amazon.com.*

[4] See *The Marshmallow Test: Mastering Self-Control* by Walter Mischel.

[5] Excerpted from *Shrink Your Stress in 5 Steps* by Jedd Hafer (2014). *Amazon.com.*

MORE POSITIVE MESSAGES
FROM THE AUTHORS.

WWW.ELEVATEPUB.COM

elevate
publishing

DELIVERING TRANSFORMATIVE MESSAGES
TO THE WORLD

Visit www.elevatepub.com for our latest offerings.

NO TREES WERE HARMED IN THE MAKING OF THIS BOOK.

OK, so a few did make the ultimate sacrifice.

In order to steward our environment, we are partnered with *Plant With Purpose*, to plant a tree for every tree that paid the price for the printing of this book.

To learn more, visit www.elevatepub.com/about

PLANT WITH PURPOSE | WWW.PLANTWITHPURPOSE.ORG